T0208480

Rear Impact Danger

Rear Impact Danger

WARNING –
Auto Passengers & Driver Beware!

Arthur W. Hoffmann, Ed.D., P.E.

REAR IMPACT DANGER
WARNING – AUTO PASSENGERS & DRIVER BEWARE!

iUniverse books may be ordered through booksellers or by contacting:

iUniverse
1663 Liberty Drive
Bloomington, IN 47403
www.iuniverse.com
1-800-Authors (1-800-288-4677)

ISBN: 978-1-6632-0015-0 (sc)
ISBN: 978-1-6632-0016-7 (e)

Print information available on the last page.

iUniverse rev. date: 04/30/2020

This book is dedicated in honor of my Parents to whom I owe unending gratitude for the values they stood for, practiced and instilled in our family.

I also wish to thank my son, Art, Jr and Elaine for their help, support and proof-reading.

This dedication would not be complete without recognizing Carolyn, my wife, companion and friend for her support.

CONTENTS

I

INTRODUCTION

DEFINITION OF AUTOMOTIVE REAR IMPACT

The collision of two or more vehicles engaged in contact, with the rear-most vehicle (bullet) impacting, the foremost (target) vehicle(s) at a closing speed (acceleration) that results in damage (and/or) injury to occupants of all engaged vehicles.

Automotive rear impacts are the most common type of car accident, with 2.5 million occurring each year. Most often, the vehicle property damage is minor with no occupant injury. Essentially, the impact is considered as bumper-to-bumper; the occupants of each involved vehicle are alerted by the jolt of the collision. However, more serious rear impact accidents can result in life-changing events.

The purpose of this book is to inform the public of the hazards and consequences of the typical automobile rear impact that endangers all drivers and passengers experiencing this type of accident.

Most people are not aware of the significance of their seated position in the vehicle, the safety restraint systems available, or the inherent design flaws within the seats and vehicle structure. Also, the general

1

public is not knowledgeable of National Highway Transportation Safety Administration (NHTSA) and Federal Motor Vehicle Safety Standards (FMVSS), or the vehicle manufacturers' competitive models, options and safety testing protocols. These factors play an important role of ensuring the driving public's safety.

The NHTSA oversight is essential to regulating the automotive industry. The car companies and component suppliers are also obligated to assure that their products meet or exceed performance of all safety expectations. The public must also be informed about inherent hazards that may exist in the products they purchase.

The nature and function of the entire automotive industry requires that public safety be foremost in all aspects of the vehicles, requirements, testing, directions, regulation, design, enforcement and legality. Continuous industry and government oversight is needed. The above comments apply to various types of accidents, such as:

- Rear Impact (and offset)
- Frontal impact (and offset)
- Side impact (passenger and driver)
- Rollover

The information presented in this book will focus on the hazards and inherent danger in automobile accidents as a result of *rear impact*. This type of accident event involves many aspects that include the driver's and passenger's actions, knowledge of NHTSA/FMVSS requirements and government impediments, car/supplier interests, the vehicle design, safety restraint systems, and especially seating system design flaws.

II
AUTOMOTIVE SAFETY
BACKGROUND AND HISTORY

Prior to the 1960's, automobile accidents causing fatalities and serious injuries were rapidly increasing, causing public safety concern. Traffic injuries and fatalities were reported by the daily news outlets and people were demanding improved safety. Automobiles were designed and built to achieve appearance, power and speed. Safety was not a high priority. Seatbelts and other safety features were unavailable, and the public was unprotected. The interior passenger compartment was especially loaded with hazards. The dashboard and instrument panel, steering wheel, levers, sharp-edges, glass areas, hard surfaces, etc., became lethal during an accident. Door latches did not function safely. Occupant ejection was a common accident result.

In 1965, Ralph Nader published *Unsafe at Any Speed*, a critique of the safety record of the American car companies. The public outcry was immediate!

One US government agency, the General Services Administration (GSA), issued a list of proposed safety requirements that must be met prior to purchasing any future government use vehicles in 1966-1967. The automotive industry was put on notice that safety was now the top design priority going forward. This caused an unprecedented review of all potentially hazardous design features and materials to improve safety.

This was the beginning of an all-out effort resulting in today's technology advances for airbags, electronic control of vehicle maneuvers and a multitude of other safety features that save untold millions of lives and prevent debilitating injuries The following is a brief history of the NHTSA and the initiation of U.S. automotive safety standards. On March 8, 1966 the GSA issued an extensive list of safety performance standards required for vehicles purchased by the federal government. The GSA standards were adopted and Congress established the NHTSA in 1970. During the period 1966 to 1975, the FMVSS primary crashworthiness safety standards were put into effect. These new safety standards included (**bold** indicates rear impact protection related):

1) **FMVSS 201 – Occupant Protection in Interior Impact - 1967**
2) **FMVSS 202 – Head Restraints – 1968 and 202a rev - 2009**
3) FMVSS 203 – Impact Protection for Driver from Steering Control - 1967
4) FMVSS 204 – Steering Control Rearward Displacement - 1967
5) FMVSS 205 – Glazing Materials - 1967
6) FMVSS 206 – Door Locks and Door Retention Components - 1967
7) **FMVSS 207 – Seating Systems - 1967, Multi-Purpose Vehicles (MPVs), Trucks - 1972**
8) **FMVSS 208 – Occupant Crash Protection - 1967**
9) **FMVSS 209 – Seat Belt Assemblies - 1967**
10) **FMVSS 210 – Seat Belt Assembly Anchorages - 1967**
11) FMVSS 212 – Windshield Mounting - 1968
12) **FMVSS 213 – Child Restraint Systems - 1970**
13) **FMVSS 225 – Child Restraint Anchorage Systems - 2009**

Since the inception of the various FMVSS standards, numerous revisions and upgrades were made in many of the requirements to reflect current technology, testing and accident data. However, FMVSS 207 Seating Systems, the primary standard relating to occupant seat safety, has **never** been revised to reflect the collapsing seatback phenomenon. This dangerous structural seat design hazard is present in virtually all passenger vehicles to this day. Millions of unknowing occupants have been killed or severely injured as a result of seatback failure due to rear impact accidents.

III
FMVSS 207 – Seating Systems

FMVSS 207 establishes requirements for seats, their attachment assemblies, and installation, to minimize the possibility of failure as a result of forces on the seat in a collision impact. The standard applies to all seating positions including second and third-row seats. Seats perform a similar function as seatbelts, that is, restraining the occupant in the seat during a collision. There are two aspects, the vehicle seat system and the seat adjusters.

- Vehicle Seat System - A structure engineered to seat the driver and passengers that includes all cotton and foam rubber padding material, trim material, decorative metal trim parts, seat adjusters and supporting components.
- Seat Adjusters - Devices anchored to the vehicle floor pan which support the seat frame and provides seat assembly fore and aft adjustment. This includes any track, link, or power actuating assemblies necessary to adjust the longitudinal and vertical seat position.

This standard specifies the minimum strength requirements which must be met (or exceeded) to secure the safety of the vehicle occupants (passengers). **The basic requirements are for any position to which the seat can be adjusted:**

(a) Twenty times the weight of the seat applied in a forward longitudinal direction, at the center of gravity (CG).
(b) Twenty times the weight of the seat applied in a rearward longitudinal direction, at the CG.
(c) For a seat belt attached to the seat, the forces imposed on the seat by the seat belt are applied simultaneously with the forces in (a) and (b) above.
(d) In its rearmost position – a force that produces a 3,300 in-lb. (373 Nm.) moment (torque) about the seating reference point for each designated seating position that the seat provides, applied to the upper cross-member of the seatback in a rearward longitudinal direction.
(e) Seats should remain in the adjusted position during the application of each force.

To comply with these requirements, seats are subjected to a FMVSS 207 Laboratory Test Procedure developed by the Office of Vehicle Safety Compliance (OVSC). The testing protocol is a static force simulation to meet the above requirements. FMVSS 207 does not require a dynamic test simulation (except for a folding seatback locking device).

The 3,300 in.lb. moment (torque) requirement is the most controversial requirement; not because of its severity, but due to its simplicity (ease of compliance because of the low- threshold of meeting this requirement). For example, actual testing of the 3,300 in-lb. requirement demonstrated that a typical (tubular construction) "lawn chair" meets the 3,300 in-lb. requirement. However, this FMVSS requirement is a minimum requirement. It can be exceeded at the will of the Original Equipment Manufacturer (OEM) car companies (seat manufacturers/designers). Currently, most OEM car companies have chosen to increase the 3,300 in-lb. moment (torque) requirements by a multiple of two to three times (average = 9,500 in-lbs.). This has strengthened the typical seatback structure, reducing the incidence of whiplash occurrences at lower-speed rear impacts. However, this has not raised the threshold to significantly reduce or eliminate the seat collapse phenomenon. FMVSS 301 Fuel System Integrity (Rear Moving Barrier Test) with a 50th % tile driver dummy (not instrumented or measured) indicates that the dissipated energy of the crash and seat-structure load to be in the 20,000 to 30,000 in-lb. range.

The original FMVSS 207 (1967) requirements have remained unchanged with no revisions to the current date. The controversy between "Rigid versus Yielding" seats has continued for over 60 years and continues today. Public concern is due to consequences of common rear impact crashes.

IV
REAR-IMPACT CONSEQUENCES

There are two major injury types caused by rear impact accidents, (1) whiplash (non-lethal injury) and (2) seat collapse (potential lethal Injury).

Whiplash injury is the result of instantaneous acceleration of the head/neck resulting in non-fatal stretching (twisting) and severe stiffness of the upper torso. This most often occurs at lower-speed rear impacts. Whiplash can be a very painful injury that may require a neck brace over a long healing period. Typically, this treatment is costly and often covered by medical insurance, further increasing the financial cost of rear impacts.

The FMVSS 202 Head Restraints standard introduced in 1968, and 202a (effective in 2009), reduced the number of whiplash events. The FMVSS 202a revision allowed various new versions of head restraint designs. Car companies developed and implemented improved whiplash systems such as passive designs that activate and automatically adjust the head restraint to enhance the potential whiplash performance for the front passenger and driver positions. There are both manual and automatic versions of these "active" systems. Many of the new head restraint systems include electronic controls and rear impact sensing features effective for limiting whiplash injuries since the 2009 model year. The focus on the consequences of whiplash has diminished and is now directed toward seat-collapse design issues.

Seat Collapse injuries are far more serious and can involve both front and rear seat occupants. The collapsing seatback can entrap rear-seated passengers, causing crushing injury and potential death. Compliance with FMVSS 207 requirements is intended to ensure that the ultimate strength of the seat structure is adequate to meet foreseeable automobile usage and driving events. This would include car-to-car crashes that occur at both low and higher speeds. The collapsing seat issue often occurs at closing speeds above 20 mph.

The failure mode typically is at the intersection (junction) of the seat cushion and the seatback, assuming the seat structure is symmetrically loaded. The forces generated in a rear impact cause the driver and/or front occupant to accelerate rearward into the seatback, resulting in rearward deformation (reclining) at the pivot joint-to-cushion. This results in a ramping posture of the seated occupant. Depending upon the occupant's weight and rear impact forces, the seatback collapses rearward and the occupant can be ejected into the vehicle's rear compartment. The occupant ramping that occurs also causes the seat belt to lose retention and the person can slide under the seat belt. This phenomenon is termed "seat collapse".

The typical rear crash involves an errant driver impacting the vehicle directly in front of his/her vehicle. The impacted vehicle was stopped or slowly moving relative to the speed of the impacting vehicle. Occupants of both vehicles are at risk, but the driver and occupants of the impacted vehicle are in far more danger. The front seat occupants are subject to the seat back reclining rearward rapidly with the driver losing control of the vehicle.

Front Seat Collapse

However, an even more dangerous situation is the entrapment of the rear-seated passengers, especially children. NHTSA standards (and state laws) require young children to be seated in the rear of the vehicle. This includes infants and younger children occupying child restraint systems (CRS). A seat collapse that leads to the entrapment of a child can cause serious or fatal injuries. Unfortunately, this happens far too many times. NHTSA data analysis (by Friedman Research Corporation) shows that over the 1990 to 2014 period nearly 900 children seated behind a front-seated occupant, or in a center-rear seat, died in rear impacts of 1990 and later model-year cars.

Rear-end crashes are the second most common vehicle accidents. NHTSA, car companies and the U.S. Congress have been aware of the inherent hazards of faulty seat design since the original FMVSS 207 Seating Systems design standard was issued in 1967. This ineffective standard sets inadequate requirements for the structural strength of automotive seat systems. The standard is intended to be the minimum strength requirement. Car companies and designers have the option to exceed a standard requirement if they believe it serves the public good. They seldom take the initiative because of cost and other considerations.

V
RIGID VERSUS YIELDING SEATBACK STRUCTURE

Over the years, there has been much controversy regarding seat strength (rigid) versus (yielding) of the seatback-to-cushion structure design.

Advocates of "yielding seat structure" believe that the seatback should absorb crash energy, reducing the effective force on the driver or front seat passenger and avoiding potential injury to the seated occupant. Advocates of the "rigid seat design" believe that the seat should remain in its upright position to avoid loss of control and to maintain effective seat and shoulder belt restraint. A compromise between these two viewpoints is required. The seatback should not appear to be a very visible failure on inspection following the accident, but be designed to absorb the crash energy internally to reduce the forces on the occupants

   a) Limit the recline angle of the seatback to avoid rear passenger entrapment.
   b) The reclining seatback should absorb the head/body energy forces of rear impact, restricting the HIC (head injury criteria) to a safe level.
   c) Limit seat and vehice deformation (intrusion) of the front compartment to avoid loss of vehicle control.
   d) Limit rigidity (firmness) of the entire seat structure and trim to reduce impact forces on the driver and front passenger.

Seat Back Common Failure

A very rigid (firm) driver/passenger front seat is simple to design and build (with added structure). However, the result in any accident mode would be detrimental to all occupants because a rigid seat would lack of energy management and not absorb/dissipate the high impact forces.

Since the enactment of FMVSS 207 in 1967, the flawed 3,300 in-lb. torque requirement has generated the Rigid versus Yielding seat controversy. Car companies, and their seat manufacturers, used the FMVSS 207 requirements to design and certify their seat systems. Almost immediately, rear impact accidents demonstrated the shortcomings of the FMVSS 207 requirements. People killed and injured due front seat failure (seatback collapse) filed lawsuits against the car companies. The defense attorneys responded with the "rigid seat" claim. The plaintiffs' case was based on the obvious evidence, the accident seat. The defense was the FMVSS 207 requirements allowing yielding beyond the 3,300 in-lb. requirement (to absorb energy). The adversaries were identified; car companies versus the trial lawyers (representing the injured public). The Rigid versus Yielding seat controversy continues today.

Since 1967 there have been millions of severe car seat injuries, including many fatalities of motor vehicle occupants due to rear-end crashes. NHTSA knew about the flawed FMVSS 207 requirements from the beginning and has failed to resolve the issues. NHTSA administrators are replaced on a frequent basis, with most of them unqualified political appointees. Over many years, safety advocates have petitioned NHTSA to do something to rectify the shortcomings of FMVSS 207 requirements with specific modifications to enhance the safety of rear-end collision performance. For example, increase the 3,300 in-lb. torque requirements to a 20,000 to 30,000 range and include dynamic testing similar to the FMVSS 301 Rear Moving Barrier Test requirement.

As recently as March 2016, the Center for Automotive Safety, petitioned NHTSA to "take action to protect children riding in the rear seats of vehicles from the risk of being killed or severely injured when struck by a collapsing front seatback in a rear-end crash." The petition asks NHTSA to warn parents as follows:

> **If Possible, Children Should be Placed in Rear Seating Positions Behind Unoccupied Front Seats. In Rear-End Crashes, the Backs of Occupied Front Seats are Prone to Collapse Under the Weight of Their Occupants. If This Occurs, the Seatbacks and Their Occupants Can Strike Children in Rear Seats and Cause Severe or Fatal Injuries.**

The petition states, "The problem underlying the need for the warnings sought by petitioner is, of course, the poor performance of seatbacks in rear-end crashes, and of serious inadequacy of the federal motor vehicle standard, FMVSS 207, which specifies minimum seat and seatback performance levels." Attached to the petition is a timeline, "Collapsing Seatbacks And Injury "Causation: A Timeline Of Knowledge," which summarizes "the history of manufacturer and NHTSA inaction to ensure that in rear-end crashes, front seats provide adequate protection not only for their occupants but for people in the rear seats behind them."

Separately, the Center for Automotive Safety (CAS) filed a detailed analysis of lawsuits, police reports and litigated cases showing the dangers of seatback collapse are far greater than what the agency recognizes. Seatback collapse is not captured by the Fatality Analysis Reporting System (FARS) database on which the agency has relied for all too long to deny there is a seatback collapse danger. FARS does not provide any information on seatback collapse. Out of sixty-four seatback collapse death and injury crashes, the center only found two where the police report referenced seatback because of the seat failure.

For many years NHTSA has urged parents to. place children in the rear seats of cars because of the risk that, in the front seat, they might be injured by inflating airbags in frontal crashes.

But the petition notes that the "unintended consequences" of this policy has been to "expose them to another kind of hazard – that of being struck or crushed when the back of a front seat occupied by an adult, collapses rearward …", concluding that, "Until cars on the American highway are equipped with adequately strong front seats and seatbacks, children in rear seats behind occupied front seats will continue to be in danger of death or severe injury from seatback failures in rear-end impacts."

The petition reports on an analysis of NHTSA data (by Friedman Research Corporation) done at the Center's request. **The analysis shows that over the twenty-four-year period of 1990 to 2014, nearly 900 children seated behind a front-seat occupant or in a center rear seat died in rear impacts of 1990 and later model-year cars.**

As the timeline shows, NHTSA has frequently been alerted to the hazards of weak designs and inadequate federal performance standards for seats and seatbacks. "Papers published by the Society of Automotive Engineers as early as 1967 described the need for adequate front-seat crashworthiness in graphic and alarming terms. A poorly designed car seat 'becomes an injury-producing agency during collision,' said one. Another stated,'… a weak seatback is not recognized as an acceptable solution for motorist protection from rear-end collisions."

In 1974, the petition notes, NHTSA announced its intention to develop a new standard "covering the total seating system" and requiring dynamic rear-impact crash testing. But thirty years later, in 2004, it abandoned the plan, saying it needed "additional research and data analysis", leaving in place the woefully weak requirements of the FMVSS 207 standard which has not been upgraded since its adoption in 1967.

In its conclusion, the petition states that warning parents of the hazards of front seatback collapse to children in the rear seat is an essential measure "made necessary by the continued absence of a federal motor vehicle safety standard requiring that cars be equipped with adequately protective front seats." The agency "can take most of the requested steps on its own, without time-consuming rulemaking, and should do so promptly."

The CAS petition includes a timeline describing the inaction of NHTSA, Congress and car companies to ignore this outrageous public safety hazard, as follows:

1) 1967 – Society of Automotive Engineers (SAE) papers issued a memorandum stating

2) that a weak seat (structure) is unacceptable for motorist protection in a rear-end collision.

3) Over the years, safety advocates and consumer organizations petitioned NHTSA to address the collapsing seat issues to no avail until 1974.

4) 1974 - In answer to the various consumer petitions, NHTSA announced its intention to develop a new standard covering the "total seating system" and require dynamic rear impact crash testing. However, thirty years later in 2004, they abandoned the plan saying it needed "additional research and analysis".

5) 1989 – ARCCA Engineering Inc. issued a petition to amend 49 CFR 571.207, FMVSS 207 Seating Systems. Stating that FMVSS 207 is nothing more than a **Static** standard for the **empty** seat structure without any consideration during a rear-end crash. The petition was denied.

6) 2015 – The same ARCCA petition was updated and reissued to NHTSA with no response.

7) 2016 – CAS Executive Director Clarence Ditlow petitioned NHTSA to do something about the collapsing-seat issue. In the petition, the CAS informed NHTSA of the following facts:

- Since, 2001, FARS-based data stated that an anmual average of **fifty (50)** children riding in the backseat have been killed in rear collisions.
- They listed 64 lawsuits relative to seat-collapse, involving death and severe injury included 22 children.

NHTSA failed to respond to the petition.

As of 2020 MVSS 207 remains unrevised, and front seat collapse in rear-end crashes continues to this day.

The lawsuits also continue with multi-million dollar penalties and settlements. Virtually all car companies were represented in major litigation due to seat failure in rear-end collisions.

Example penalty/settlement costs include: several reported (plaintiff v defendant) legal-cases.

Car Company	Penalty/Settlement
Audi/VW	$124.0 million
Toyota (Lexus)	$242.0 million
GM/Chevrolet	$43.1 million
Chrysler / Neon	$43.1 million

Many more settlements for undisclosed amounts were concluded and kept confidential. The legal system, attorneys and car companies purposely withhold this information from the general public uninformed. Therefore, specific safety defects are unknown, except for official NHTSA product recalls. Numerous lawsuits continue today. NHTSA and the car companies fail to offer safety initiatives and requirements to enhance FMVSS 207 Seating Systems to reduce seat collapse injuries.

VI
SEAT STRENGTH RESEARCH

Beginning in the early 1960's, car companies were aware of rear impact accidents and the resulting injuries and deaths due to structural seat and anchorage failure. Tragedies were only expected in high speed crashes but not at low speed bumper-to-bumper type events. Seat strength and seat anchorage was unregulated. Comfort, endurance (wear) and cost were the goals of seating design.

The seat structure was very similar within the automotive industry, with trim-type and material were the primary seating differences. Beginning in 1967, with the introduction of the first GSA requirements and following the establishment of NHTSA, car companies were required to meet the new standards and test certification for the specific requirements of FMVSS 207 Seating Systems. Up to that point, competition had ruled, with car companies producing seats to internal company design standards. There were no comprehensive industry standards.

The automotive industry now had standards to follow and they did. Unfortunately, FMVSS 207 requirements were not founded on basic engineering principles, research data, or test verification. NHTSA was a new bureaucracy, not familiar with the automotive industry and politically motivated. Over the next few years, it was evident that the FMVSS strength requirements were flawed due to the rising casualties and severe injuries from rear-end collisions. NHTSA became a target of criticism by both car companies and the legal establishment. Seat strength versus energy absorption during a rear impact became the focus of attention.

Fundamental engineering research became a priority within all areas of the automotive industry. The immediate research effort was to define the concerns related to rearend crashes and the injury potential, as follows:

a) Whiplash (not a lethal injury) - The solutions were to raise the seatback height (vision concern) and implementation of the FMVSS 202 and 202a Head Restraint System requirements in (1967) and (2009) respectively.
b) Collapsing seatback (potentially lethal injury) — the concerns were occupant ramping, potential ejection, head impact hazards, and rear occupant entrapment.

All of the above concerns and potential solutions were topics of intense research over many years and investigation continues today.

In the early 1960s, General Motors was the prominent car company to test various theories and established a basic understanding of rear-end crashes and potential injury results. As an engineer at the GM Fisher Body Division, the author was involved in the dynamic Hydraulic-Controlled Gas-Energized) (HYGE) sled testing to benchmark the pros/cons of various design alternatives for seatback strength in simulated rear impact levels with 95th percentile and 50th percentile instrumented dummies. For example:

Impact Speed (Miles per Hour)	Result
10 and below (low speed)	Whiplash injury
10 to 20	Seatback failure and loss of driver control
20 to 30	Ramping rearward
30 to 50	Ejection into rear compartment and rear occupant entrapment

Proposed seat system design and ideas were explored, such as strong rigid seat, high back versus headrest, various yielding strength alternatives, controlled tipping seat, etc. As time went on, actual rear-end crash data accumulated allowing research scientists and engineers to develop realistic solutions to the collapsing seatback issue. Progress was made in understanding the Rigid versus Yielding alternatives. The conclusion was that an unyielding rigid seat is not a solution. A well designed energy-absorbing seat structure with energy absorbing (EA) trim was the answer.

In the early 1990s, GM researchers David Viano and Dick Neeley developed a new test method termed "quasi-static and dynamic tests" to determine the potential benefits and risks of current seatback strength and seatback system alternative designs. Using this new technology, they developed a "high retention seat system" designed to keep the occupants in the seat during a rear-end collision. The GM Inland Fisher Guide Division and Delphi Division finalized a safer seat design marketed "the Catcher's Mitt" and "Flex Width Seat". This design controlled the energy transfer from the occupant to the trim and energy-absorbing padding of the seat. The debate over the safety of Rigid versus Yielding seats was put to rest.

Two GM divisions worked jointly together to develop this new seat system. The author was assigned to Inland Fisher Guide Division, responsible for the seat adjusters and mechanical components, Dick Neeley worked at the Delphi Division responsible for the seat design and assembly, and David Viano, a GM research scientist developed the seat frame structure using the new testing technology. The focus of the "high-retention seat system" was to solve the collapsing seat phenomenon as a result of rear-end collisions. However, other aspects such as _occupant positioning_ would surface in the future.

Typical Sled Test (HYGE)

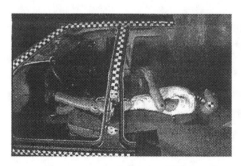

Dummy Ramping -Sled Test

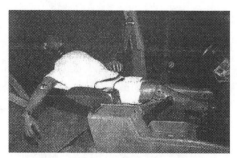

Dummy Ramping -Sled Test

Once GM introduced the "high retention seat", other car companies adopted their version of the design. However, it was not universal. Even within GM, not all of their brands utilized the new seat technology in all vehicles. This was due to cost, vehicle size, and model-year changeover. The entire global market is a mix of various seat structural designs. BMW, Mercedes and Volvo have stronger designs, as do other car companies that offer all-belts-to-seat (ABTS) restraint systems. FMVSS 207 requirements remain unchanged. The incidence of collapsing seatbacks due to rear impact accidents is lessened, but they still occur and so do the injuries as well as the lawsuits. The GM "high retention seat" is certainly a positive improvement in solving the structural aspect of rear-end collisions, but not a cure-all. There are other contributing factors that have not been adequately addressed.

VII
FRONT SEAT OCCUPANT POSITION

In a recent inspection of a vehicle and seat system that was involved in a high-speed rear impact, several new concerns were identified. The vehicle a (2005 Ford Explorer) was impacted on left-rear-side in a skewed (offset) direction with large crush occurring on the driver's side. There were two occupants. The passenger was a 180 lb. male (uninjured). The driver was a short, average weight female (fatally injured). The passenger was seated with the manual adjuster in mid-fore-aft position. The driver scat had an 8-way power seat adjuster. Her position was full-forward, full-up and tilted rearward (front-up and rear-down).

The inspection of the vehicle and seats was conducted by both plaintiff and defense experts. The seats were stripped down (no trim) with the complete frame and adjusters. They were out of the vehicle and viewed side-by-side. Several interesting observations were noted, as follows:

a) The front passenger seatback collapsed in a typical mode-of-failure, with a tubular back frame crimped at the junction of the back-to-cushion structure. No other deformation or breakage was observed. The anti-submarine ramp of the cushion structure was also undamaged.

b) The driver's seatback was only partially reclined (permanent set). However, the occupant was ejected, indicating greater dynamic recline. The 8-way power adjuster linkage was severely deformed and twisted toward the inboard-side. Due to the linkage design, the driver was in a poor-position to resist the rear impact forces.

c) The driver's anti-submarine ramp was also deformed, indicating that it functioned as designed. This anti-ramp panel, integrated into the seat-cushion structure, is designed to keep a smaller occupant from sliding-under the seatbelt during a front or rear collision.

d) The most important finding of the inspection was the diverse failure modes of the passenger seat versus the driver seat.

- The passenger seat failure was a typical acute crimping (tubular bending) of the seatback frame at the junction of the cushion structure. This is the common failure mode of "seat collapse" that results from a rear-end collision.

- The driver's seat failure was the result of the 8-way power seat adjuster design. The articulating linkage deformed and absorbed the crash energy as well as the occupant's acceleration forces. Due to the selected power-adjusted position, the driver experienced the seat and mechanism deformation forces over a longer period than the passenger.

e) The result of this rear impact inspection indicates that the occupant's seated position may have a profound effect on the result of a rear-end collision.

f) All "collapsing seat" research to-date only focused on the actual seat structure and the 'Rigid versus Yielding" phenomenona of the "high retention seat" design ("Catcher's Mitt") may not be appropriate for multi-adjustable seats or power adjusters. Seat adjustment and occupant position were not a consideration while researching the "collapsing" seat issue.

VIII
ADJUSTABLE SEAT SYSTEMS

FMVSS 207 Defines "seat adjuster" as the part of the seat assembly that provides forward and rearward positioning of the seat bench and back, and/or rotation around a vertical axis, including any fixed portion, such as a seat track. There are two methods of seat position adjustment, (1) manual and (2) power.

a) The typical manual seat adjuster is operated by the occupant using spring-assisted levers with handles and/or, knobs to change the fore-aft, vertical (up/down) or recline seat position to achieve comfort. Generally, manual adjusters are utilized where cost is a priority.

b) Power seat adjusters are far more complex. They are designated as 2-way, 4-way, 6-way, or 8-way (for seatback recline). The adjustment modes are powered by multiple motors dependent on the function and design. The articulation can be a linkage system, power-screw or hydraulic. Power adjusters are typically optional equipment.

Over the years, power seat adjusters have become increasingly popular for both the passenger front seat and the driver seat. Therefore, occupant position has become an important safety factor affecting the outcome when the vehicle is impacted in any direction.

ARTHUR W. HOFFMANN, ED.D., P.E.

Designers of power seat adjuster systems should consider the safety of the occupant in determining the extent-of-movement various adjustment modes allow, and the resulting position of the occupant during different crash situations. <u>Occupant positioning</u> should be a safety research priority in addition to the structural Rigid versus Yielding investigation that occurred over the past years.

8-Way Power Adjuster

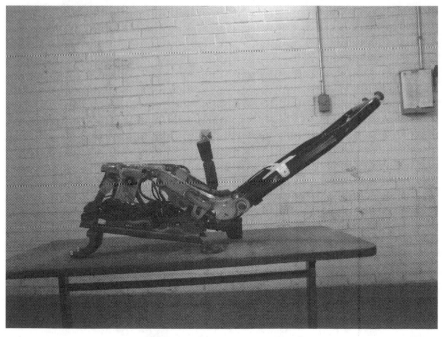

Deformed Power Seat Back

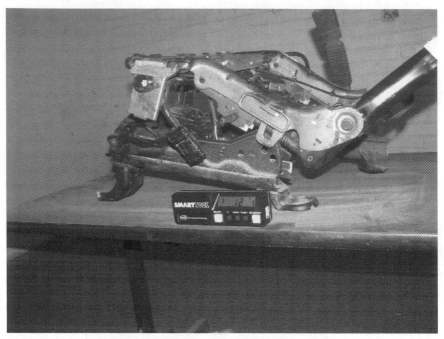

Deformed Power Adjuster-Side View

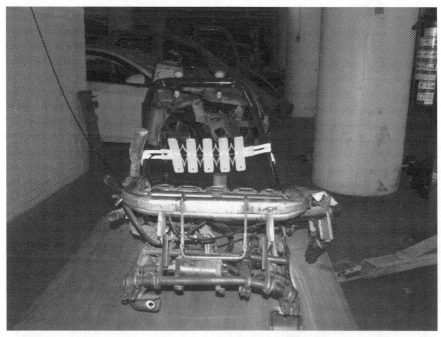

Deformed Power Seat -Front View

Deformed Power Seat -Front View

Power Adjuster Failure- CloseUp

Manual Seat Back Failure

IX
TESTING PROTOCOL AND CERTIFICATION

Car companies are obligated to consider the impact on public safety when they introduce complex features or options, such as multi-adjustment seats that may endanger the occupant. The adjustment parameters (movement of the seat, fore-aft, height and tilt) require that the occupant position meets human-factor limits. The testing protocol and certification should ensure consideration of worst-case (adjustment extremes) be the criteria and should include vehicle impact (front, rear and side) safety considerations,

FMVSS 207 SEATING SYSTEMS:

The front seated occupants, especially the driver, require special consideration due to vehicle control and proper response to accidental impact. Seatbelt retention can be compromised when a rear impact causes the occupant's recline position to exceed the current comfort setting.

FMVSS 207 addresses the importance of occupant position and the certification testing protocol. The general performance test requirements for each occupant seat shall withstand the following forces.

a) **<u>In any position to which it can be adjusted</u>** – Twenty times the mass of the seat in a forward and rearward longitudinal direction.

b) For a seatbelt assembly attached to the seat, an additional 3,000 lb. (lap-belt) force is applied simultaneously to (a), see (above).

c) **<u>In the seat's rearmost position</u>** – A force that produces a 3,300 in-lb. (373 N-m) moment about the seating reference point, applied to the upper seatback cross-member in a rearward longitudinal direction.

Each seat shall remain in its adjusted position when tested.

FMVSS 207 strength requirements are "static" laboratory tests. Dynamic testing with dummies would be more appropriate for solving the "collapsing seat" phenomenon due to rear-end crashes.

X

OTHER REAR IMPACT DANGER – THIRD-ROW SEATING

Second and third-row seat positions are also susceptible to collapse during rear-end collisions. This is especially applicable to the third-row that is very close to the point-of impact. FMVSS 207 requirements apply to all seating positions and rear seats also collapse in rear impacts. The forgoing discussion focused on the driver and passenger front seats due to loss-of-vehicle control and the endangerment of rear seat occupants. Therefore, the front seats were the subject of the "collapsing-seat research.

In past years, third-row seating was primarily offered in the larger vans and the longer sport utility vehicles (SUVs) that had enough crush space to absorb much of the impact energy. The 3-point belt system anchorage location and routing also offered superior restraint.

Recently, many vehicles have been downsized due to fuel efficiency standards and cost. This continuing trend for smaller SUVs and crossovers compromise passenger seating capacity. To meet customer demand for third-row seating, car companies are squeezing third-row seats into these vehicles barely long enough to accommodate them, leaving mere inches between the seat and the back of the vehicle. For example, GM's Buick Rendezvous, a crossover SUV has just eight inches between the third-row seatback and the tailgate glass. Ford's Explorer SUV has thirteen inches. Honda's Acura MDX has about twelve inches, depending on how the seat is adjusted. For comparison, GM's Chevy Suburban has thirty-six inches.

Adults won't even fit many of these latest third-row seat designs. Therefore, when occupied, the passengers are likely to be children. Children are least likely to be correctly, compounding the danger. Space (distance) is not the only criterion for judging the safety of third-row seats; seat strength and vehicle design are also involved. Crash energy management of rear-end collisions is vital to absorb and dissipate the forces. Third-row seats in these mini-size SUVs and vans lack the space and vehicle structure to provide any reasonable crash energy management. Accident statistics show that third-row seats in these vehicles are about twice as dangerous as other seating positions.

There were 2.3 million rear-end collisions in the year 2000, or 21.7 % of all crashes, with fatalities in 2,980 accidents. With the continuing proliferation of these small vehicles with third-row seats, injuries and deaths will increase. According to a Ford Motor Company analysis, when a minivan with a third-row occupant is hit from behind, the occupant is killed half the time. It's lucky then, that third rows are infrequently occupied- just 1% or 2% of the time.

Car companies are well-aware of the inherent danger for third-row seated occupants in these mini-size vehicles, but they continue to offer third-rows for marketing purposes. Car company CEOs know that rear-end collisions are very common, that the third-row seats will be occupied mostly by children, and their designs are substandard for safety. The third-row occupants are only inches away from a potential crushing impact. Children will be killed and severely injured. It is unconscionable for the car companies to offer this predictable safety hazard. The public is not informed of the safety consequences of third-row seats and especially allowing children to occupy them.

NHTSA continues to avoid addressing the entire automotive seating safety issues inherent in FMVSS 207 requirements and the lack of dynamic testing to ensure public safety.

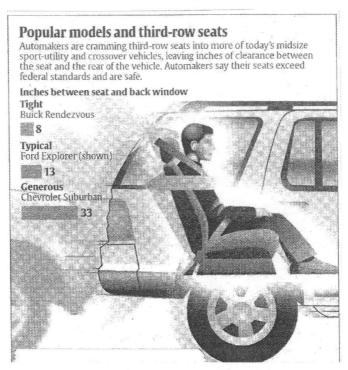

Popular models and third-row seats

Automakers are cramming third-row seats into more of today's midsize sport-utility and crossover vehicles, leaving inches of clearance between the seat and the rear of the vehicle. Automakers say their seats exceed federal standards and are safe.

Inches between seat and back window

Tight
Buick Rendezvous
8

Typical
Ford Explorer (shown)
13

Generous
Chevrolet Suburban
33

3ʳᵈ Row Seat Danger

Actual Rear Impact Damage

XI
PUBLIC SAFETY INFORMATION

The general public should be aware and knowledgeable of the many hazards inherent in automotive travel and the precautions they can exercise to help ensure their personal and family safety. All vehicle passengers should protect themselves by using the restraint systems, headrest adjustment, seat adjustment, mirrors, turn signals, speed, brakes and self-positioning for their safety. It is essential that all children are correctly restrained in a CRS (child restraint system) based on their height and weight. Refer to www.safercar.gov/therightseat.

Note:

The author was involved in the development of the first child safety seat in 1967. This landmark development was the result of extensive testing at the GM Fisher Body Division proving grounds in Milford, Michigan. The introduction in the early 1960's of the (HYGE) impact sled for dynamic crash testing in the automotive industry, made possible the development of advanced occupant safety innovations. For the first time, this apparatus allowed safety researchers to simulate automobile crash forces and accelerations without destroying actual vehicles. Frontal, side and rear-impact crash test simulations were now possible. The child safety seat was one of the breakthrough products of this research. Child safety restraints (CRS) were a major development and marketed initially by GM in 1967 as the "Love Seat" and also the first rearward-facing "Infant Love Seat" in 1970. Soon after Ford introduced their "Tot-Guard" impact-table CRS.

Over time, the major seat belt companies and juvenile products manufacturers joined to develop and market various CRS models. Restraint usage is now required by all 50 states dependent on the age of the child. The expansion and use of CRS types and models has been remarkable. To meet public demand, the CRS industry has introduced a variety of innovative products to safeguard children from infants through all stages of growth until the child can be safely seated using an adult restraint (usually by 13 years of age). Currently, there are over 185 different models of CRS's on the market, manufactured by 28 independent suppliers. The CRS models include:

- Infant (rear-facing) restraints – 29 models from 14 manufacturers.
- Convertible seats – 70 models from 11 manufacturers.
- Forward facing (5-point harness) – 3 models from 3 manufacturers.
- Combination seats – 52 models from 9 manufacturers.
- Booster seats (high back and no back) – 41 models from 18 manufacturers

The CRS industry is very competitive relative to cost, quality, innovation and safety features. This has led to a very complex and confusing marketplace. Many of the restraint systems are being misused due to improper installation, confusing instruction manuals and vehicle seating differences, adaptation provisions, and correct positioning. Product recalls for design defects, faulty assembly and misinformation is prevalent in the CRS industry. Prior to purchasing any CRS model, refer to www.saferseat.gov/ease-of-use rating.

In order to combat the CRS misuse and misinformation, the "Safe-Kids Worldwide Organization" was established to reduce preventable child injuries. As a result of public demand, Congress and NHTSA created a Child Passenger Safety CPS) technician and certification training program and curriculum across America that are offering CRS fitting stations to assist parents and caregivers to properly install and use the various CRS models. These fitting stations are typically located at fire-stations, major stores and churches by Public announcement or regular bi-monthly schedule.

XII
OCCUPANT POSITIONING

A final safety issue that requires discussion is occupant positioning within the vehicle. This is important for all passengers but essential for children, especially in child restraint systems. NHTSA requires that young children sit in the rear seats of vehicles. The original reason for this restriction was due to the danger of an inflating front airbag. While it is still important for young children to be seated in the rear seat. Current model vehicles now have airbag on/off weight sensing as a safety measure to reduce small occupant danger.

GM Doesn't Leave Any Body Out!

 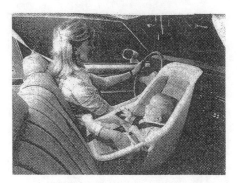

1ˢᵗ GM Child (Love) Seat

*1ˢᵗ Rearward-Facing GM
Infant (Love) Seat*

NHTSA however, has required all passenger vehicles have CRS mounting provisions in the two-out-board (Rt/Lt) rear seat positions. This CRS system is called LATCH (lower anchors and tethers for children). There are two-major concerns relative to utilizing the LATCH system. The first and foremost concern relates to side impact. The passenger/child is seated next-to-the right or left rear doors. Second, while the LATCH system offers some ease-of-use, the LATCH anchors are limited to 65 lbs. (weight of child + weight of the CRS). If the weight limit is exceeded, the vehicle seat belt must be used. The center position-of-a-rear-row seat is the most protective for any occupant. Other occupant self-positioning alternatives to enhance safety include:

a) Use the rear-center seat position if available.
b) Choose the rear seat position behind the unoccupied front seat.
c) Use the rear seat position behind the smallest (lightest) front occupant.
d) Adjust front or rear headrests to optimize protection.
e) Do not recline any seat when a vehicle is moving.
f) Always correctly fasten passenger restraints.

The above instructions should be included in the owner's manuals of the vehicle, the CRS instruction booklet and vehicle insurance directions.

References

1. Center for Auto Safety, March 9, 2016, news, NHTSA urged to warn parents of seat back failure dangers to children in rear seats.
2. The Expert Institute, February 21, 2019, article, Car seat back defect suggests potential for widespread litigation.
3. The Carlson Law Firm, September 18, 2018, personal injury post, Seat failure poses deadly risk for children in the back seat.
4. Fair Warning News, May 22, 2017, Safety,health and corporate conduct, Regulators, automakers urged to warn parents about flawed seats.
5. ARCCA Petition to NHTSA Administration, September 28, 2015, Petition to Amend FMVSS 207 – Seating Systems.
6. The Free Library (Farlex), October 5, 2019, news, Conspiracy of silence hid seat-back hazards: collapsing seat backs were a dangerous and outdated design, and GM knew it. Internal documents reveal why the automaker took so long to come up with a safer seat.
7. USA Today, September 22, 2011, article, www.orangecountylaw.com, Third row car seats may kill your kids.
8. Saunders, Molino, Kuppa – NHTSA- Paper No. 248, Performance of Seating Systems in a FMVSS No. 301 Rear Impact Crash Test.
9. Cantor A, Petition for rulemaking to amend FMVSS 207 to prohibit ramping up the seat back during a collision, NHTSA, December 28, 1989. Docket PRM-207-002.

10. Insurance Institute for Highway Safety (IIHS), http://www.hwysafety.org/vehicle_ratings/head_restraints/head.htm.

11. Prasad, P., Relationships Between Passenger Car Seat Back Strength and Injury Severity in Rear End Collisions: Field and Laboratory Studies. 973343, Society of Automotive Engineers, Inc.

12. Saczalski, K; Syson, S; Hille, R; Pozzi, M (1993): Field Accident Evaluations and Experimental Study of Seat Back Performance Relative to Rear Impact Occupant Protection. SAE 930346, Proceed, ings of the 37th Conference.

13. Saczalski KJ. Petiti1989on to Improve FMVSS 207 NHTSA, April 18, 1989. Docket PRM – 207-001 and Docket NHTSA – 1998 – 1817

14. Vino DC., "Role of the Seat in Rear Crash Safety," SAE Book, Society of Automotive Engineers, Inc., Warrendale, PA, 2002.

15. Viano, D., "Effectiveness of High-Retention Seats in Preventing Fatality: Initial Results and Trend," SAE 2003-01-1351, Society of Automotive Engineers, In., Warrendale, PA.

16. Car Seat Guidelines to Keep Your Kids Safe-(AAP Guidelines)-www.verywellfamily.com/2633328.

17. NHTSA.gov/ease of use ratings/CRS.

18. Arthur W. Hoffmann, Precious Cargo- ISBN:978-I-460-1453-8.

About the Author

Arthur W. Hoffmann, Ed.D., P.E. is a registered Professional Engineer and safety consultant. He was instrumental in the establishment of NHTSA FMVSS standards at General Motors-Fisher Body Division in the 1960's. He also developed the 1st Child Safety Seat offered by GM in 1967- "The GM Love Seat" and the initial rearward-facing "GM Infant Love Seat". He is the author three auto safety publications; "Don't be a Dummy", "Precious Cargo" and Rear-Impact Danger".

Printed in the United States
By Bookmasters